T0022912

HOT SAUCE

Kaycee Hill is a poet, creative and professional writing graduate, and digital mixed media artist. Now based near Bristol, she was born in Winchester and grew up in a working-class, mixed-heritage household – British and Caribbean – in Andover. She was selected for Poetry Ambassadors during the height of the pandemic, was a shortlisted poet for the *Poetry London* Mentoring Scheme 2020, and has been commended for her poetry by The Young Poets Network. She read her poem 'Scuffing' in the British Museum's Refugee Week YouTube event *The Poetry of Witness: Writing about Displacement, Migration and Exile* in 2021. Kaycee spent the past five years working within the healthcare sector as a domiciliary carer and as a support worker for adults with mild learning difficulties. She believes it is a role wherein you learn everything there is to know about humanity. Kaycee defines herself as an urban voyeur, with much of her urge to write taken from the spry mundanity of inner-city life. She was one of the three winners of the inaugural James Berry Poetry Prize in 2021, and her first book-length collection, *Hot Sauce*, was published by Bloodaxe Books in 2023.

KAYCEE HILL

Hot Sauce

BLOODAXE BOOKS

Copyright © Kaycee Hill 2023

ISBN: 978 1 78037 637 0

First published 2023 by
Bloodaxe Books Ltd,
Eastburn,
South Park,
Hexham,
Northumberland NE46 1BS

www.bloodaxebooks.com
For further information about Bloodaxe titles
please visit our website and join our mailing list
or write to the above address for a catalogue.

Supported using public funding by
**ARTS COUNCIL
ENGLAND**

LEGAL NOTICE

All rights reserved. No part of this book may be
reproduced, stored in a retrieval system, or
transmitted in any form, or by any means, electronic,
mechanical, photocopying, recording or otherwise,
without prior written permission from Bloodaxe Books Ltd.

Requests to publish work from this book
must be sent to Bloodaxe Books Ltd.

Kaycee Hill has asserted her right under
Section 77 of the Copyright, Designs and Patents Act 1988
to be identified as the author of this work.

Cover design: Neil Astley & Pamela Robertson-Pearce.

Printed in Great Britain by Bell & Bain Limited, Glasgow, Scotland, on
acid-free paper sourced from mills with FSC chain of custody certification.

...we are each other's
harvest:
we are each other's
business:
we are each other's
magnitude and bond.

GWENDOLYN BROOKS

ACKNOWLEDGEMENTS

Acknowledgements are due to the following publications and websites where some of these poems first appeared: *Five Dials*, *The Lost Art of Staring into Fires: Selected Poems from the University of Winchester, 2010-2022*, ed. Glenn Fosbraey (Valley Press, 2022), *Poetry Ambassadors*, *The Poetry Review* and *Young Poets' Stories*.

'Makeshift' was commended in the Poetry Society's Young Poets Network 'After Sylvia Challenge'. Kaycee Hill read 'Scuffing' in the British Museum's Refugee Week YouTube event *The Poetry of Witness: Writing about Displacement, Migration and Exile* in 2021.

Many thanks are due to Bloodaxe Books and NCLA for the James Berry Poetry Prize. I also wish to extend my deepest gratitude to Neil Astley, Sinéad Morrissey, Theresa Muñoz, Jacob Sam-La Rose and Nathalie Teitler, for making this book possible. To Malika Booker, Aviva Dautch, Carrie Etter, and all the mentors who have guided me from behind the scenes, your unwavering encouragement, insights and feedback have shaped me as a poet in immeasurable ways.

To my family, I am indebted for equipping me with the tools to write. Special thanks to my mum, for instilling a love of music and lyricism which has informed every aspect of my life. Infinite love and thanks to my sister and day one, Kiera. My muse, Tyrone Hall, for faithfully listening to each poem, attending every reading, and being my pillar of support for over a decade. To my girls – Jessica Wilson, Leah Robson and Daisy Nikoloska – who have consistently shown up for me, particularly during moments of self-doubt. I cherish you all.

Heartfelt thanks to fellow poets and writers who have graced my journey, sharing their wisdom, awareness, and talent. From you, I have learned so much. I am immensely grateful to all the poetry events that have given me the platform to share my work. And to Arts Council England for their funding, which has made all of this a reality. Thank you.

CONTENTS

FOR YOU (FOR YOU)

Muse

I'm overpowered
by desire [...] and it's all
Aphrodite's fault

SAPPHO (tr. Josephine Balmer)

From my bedroom window I turn to standing stone,
solidifying the image like a painter, or a thief.

I watch you

step off into blackness, study your hands; gloved,
fluorescent, busying the wheel –

feeling   along its scuffed teeth then pausing,
where the fingers know what they know,

used to probing the skins of peaches.

Inside the dark which dares to call itself morning
I catch your almond head, half enwrapped

by a surgical mask. Then off you go – helmeted,
camouflaged, except for the bike light
blinking

     off   *on*   *off*   *on*   *off*

on   pulsing out of the depths like plasma

and the formation of your profile gone soon after,
swallowed up by the street's unlatched jaw.

I hope that you are warm. My dressing gown
still preserves your shape.

And from our bed, as I fold in on myself, outside
glints saffron yellow, lit by electrical sentries.

A Caged Thing Freed

Your mouth slips out a sound, a sound of the world dying and reborn again,
an utterance of expanding space, time, sound flinging out of your warm

fleshy mouth, out from your pink oyster mushroom lips and for a second,
with your back burning white in the afternoon sun, you become an arctic fox

rolled over a damp mossy log. Your paw-hands dressed in skin stretch along
my many grooves like a spill, round red knuckles flushing pale at the grip.

The unfathomable patience we commit to, to prolong this shared annihilation,
to remain inside the brink. I will take my time with you – trace your temples,

your chest, every palm crease, the constellation formed inside your spine's bow,
the cool flint of your ankles. Through an open window, in the sun's fullness,

a wasp sneaks in – dusting shadows over your nose-bridge, while our bedsheets
knot themselves up. Here, I can hear your animal heart: bang bang boom.

What Love Looks Like

Skin-melded under a snarl of cover,
eclipsed by hazes of limb & bustle,

animal funk fogging the window
as we breathe in night's purples

like some huge nebulous thing,
while morning unlatches its sun

behind the cheap, broken blinds.
You taste like frenzy, sour skittles.

On leaving, your cupid's bow shoots
Aphrodite's pearl in my temple's centre

& the world's clamshell closes like an eye.

Naturalist

I check if my head is still attached to my neck –
if my heart still beats, if any teeth have let

go, unfastened from sockets, ground to powder,
fusion of rapture and ache in equal measure;

first comes sting, bliss soon after, eyes roaming
the cryptic dark of a just-surfaced fantasy.

Below, Ginuwine's *Pony* mounts the subwoofer,
chip shop vinegar cartwheels up the stairs.

I feel like I've been initiated into new territories,
like I could dip my fingers in the odd blotch

staining the mattress and paint myself with it –
bound through the village a howling thing.

A robin chimes outside. I see her bright red breast.
The thumping heart of a young, naked, ash tree.

Kitchen

This is only the second visit.
The air hums of garlic

crushed and stewed in butter
and my taste buds twitch

to taste it, muscle memory –
my small tongue salivates,

coated in phantom broth.
Sade wafts over wailing cats,

a cricket bat whacked across
blurs of ant-heads.

We're making jelly now.
As I separate the juicy cubes,

ripe with cow fat and pineapple,
her Little Bo Peep figurine

shoots me this look, crook raised,
to remind me how alien I am.

Shapeshift

My mother's brown lifelines track across
the sand of her palms, languidly joining
like barking gulls in the place where
secrets are formed or the wind speaks.

There's a face – a woman's, a graveyard
of trees or nipples pointing to Hades
dozing her stomach like roasted papayas,
and a map with clear rivers, their shells

softly turning, just to feel the sun close.
This place is ancient as comb-jelly –
where the spawning ground dances
with ideas in new combinations:

a waltz for mourning, snaking hips at war
or the mambo in love. Excavate the clag,
the clart. Make a bright star from stone
and from the mountains and the moors.

Push yourself into the valley of ghosts.
It's like the moon cracking herself open.
It's like jiving bees. A woman in the shape
of a beast, a beast in the shape of a woman.

The Collector

She comes to me, every night
at the stroke of three, well fitted in her
black and her white, to greet me.

She taps twice, two for joy –
with her pointed matte, black beak
and drops from her tongue
treasure, onto my windowsill.

She brings flecks of silver foil, beads
from necklaces passed, beer
coloured glass and sometimes when
she is feeling generous, gold.

She is a strange creature, beautiful in
her plumage, her ink blue tail-stripe
winking as she turns to feed, I
am certain she likes me watching her.

She eats her fill and when she is done
shoots her beady, liquid topaz eye into
mine and flies into the shrieking wind.

Dreams of Home

Bare bottles of tonic wine line the windowsill.
     Goes down too damn easy – he says – *like medicine,*
his voice lagging, thickening to cherry syrup.
     Homesickness is a symptom of displacement,
separation, a meditation on our foundations.
     Ah, Jamaica! He travels there in a boat of smoke –
mi soon come… mi soon come… figures or spirits
     swim throughout the brain-grey of his eyelids
where everything is in a state of becoming.
     & when my grandfather, the innate sailor,
reaches the shore, he moors himself to a small black sun.
     Souls break open among ripened mangoes
& black-billed parrots, the root aroma of yams
     shucked back, disclosing all that yellow flesh –
still, Jamaica pains him…*like a new bruise pressed.*
     Over there, on glaring white sand, his young love
picking out her dreadlocks with a limestone comb.
     He roams barefoot. Reaches an ackee tree budding
golden rings & reams of trawl net baked into bones.
     Jah, free my skin… free my mind… my body…
Below a colossal canopy of yellow, black & green, a boy
     with my grandfather's face sleeps soundly;
harvesting mislaid memories like queen conch pearls.

Ghost

(for Aaron Bowman)

Behind a car window soupy with breath and chill
a gilded-haired boy-man is doubled over,

in prayer or pain it's hard to tell. Through the veil
his expression matches one of god's only son;

drooping head and eyelids padlocked – mouth open
slightly as if he's bound to speak in the gift

of tongues or rap along to Kendrick's new album,
articulating lyrical melodies in blistering speed,

full throttle in his seat, anyone in their right mind
could easily confuse that boy for the radio.

Scores of memories sat on the passenger side: Kano–
J Hus–Bugzy Malone tearing the speaker wide;

driving village roads and going nowhere in particular,
sun squinting at the fat face of your watch.

For the Hive

You're an effigy in the cleft of a tree.
A cosmic Fabergé egg pulsing –

some sort of puzzling fruit hanging
from lightning-fractured limbs.

Assembly of bronze and pitch your
hexagonal fortress brims alive,

unphased by the opinions of lessers,
turning inside the wind's mouth.

O how you stir like Medusa's locks,
click-clacking, a Shamanka's rattle.

Scuffing

I picture my mother at eleven years old –

  bow-legged, pint-sized, confined in her uniform,
eyes weary even then, pulled in at the corners,
    cast in hickory, flecked with gold,

  the same shade Diana Ross & the Supremes wore
on the cover of *Cream of the Crop*, shook those hips in.

Gappy teeth, freckled cheeks, walking home from school,
  dragging new Clarks against salmagundi brick,

their leather-cracked cry trailing behind
  like the music of a cabasa made from gourd,
like bay leaves laughing, rice and peas boiling.

I see her enjoying the scuffing, revelling in its wrongness –

the desecration of shoes so dismally British, so hideous,
mouth flung open to the sky, armed to the back teeth
  with glee and remembering

that pot of Kiwi black polish under the sink, that'll slide over
  the damage like shea butter.

I see her playing out the trouble she'd be in, hearing it
  like an echo in an aluminium can,
    Great-Nanny's voice rearing up

over the ruins, the crime scene,

  then simmering down to a tiny puff of steam
because she's eleven, grown, a God –

The Gift

We take the passing of confectionery very seriously
in my family. Mum eats rock slow, slow,

she twists bows of plastic, won't rush to unwrap it,
pushes out the rock's white tattooed head
and works at it like a whetstone.

Her mouth drones. The sound of gratitude –
of memories plunging in: first time away,

hands rummaging through a crate of crab toys
and shapeshifting fish magnets,

stopping stock-still at multitudes of candied rock
almost violent in their prismatic pigments,
grinning in pristine rows,

50p burning in her palm like a glob of molten rock
as she makes her choice of aniseed and cherry.

In our lineage we were destined for sweetness –
a verb hiding in the mouth of an oyster.

I kissed the stick of rock twice before posting it.
A young seagull called out for its mother.

Last Shift at St Wins

You laugh as I hold out my hands,
        my blue plastic-wrapped fingers,

        and try a few aimless notes,
vowels bouncing all around us,

        a mirage of floating faces
                reflected in white tile.

You look over me
        with your small ripe eyes,
                those ruinous black pupils,

        creased lids pulsing
like you're trying to say something.

        I'm listening – I'm listening –
but I'm still unable to decode the message

and you cup your wilting hands
        into ramekins,
                one for each of us,

as if to say: I know you see me
                  I see you too

MY GEOGRAPHIES

Polystyrene Cup

Once, we drove to the nature reserve
and watched from our seats as frogs went
piggybacking from pond to pond.

I dropped my polystyrene cup out the window.
It was scarred with fingernail indents
and lipstick bruises.

You bust-a-gut laughing as it melted.

The radio fidgeted with static.

A SIDE

I always remember exactly what I was doing, where I was,
and what the record meant to me

GOLDIE

It wafts over me like second-hand smoke. Like a dream heaved
from a stranger's throat & contained inside my own. Back then
language was merely chopped into bites of sound: the babble &
chirps of a simple animal, before teeth protruded through gums.
My footprints score a diagonal path in the council-shag carpet,
it feels like walking on snow. I climb into my mumma's throne;
she's carved from brown-gold stone, tough stuff, smoky geode.
Place my arms over hers & inhale the musk of her unswerving
back – Palmer's cocoa butter mixed with the twang of roll-ups.
Night plasters over everything. Turns the windows into mirrors.
The needle in daddy's fingers glints as if crafted by some magic.
Flash of silver under black – the moon's hangnail. It scratches.
Spins. Jolts. Pops. Hisses. A breath. The music encompasses
us as we huddle in the front room, enfolded like a modest pride.
& far away, or far in, someplace else, a voice declares: *reload!*

B SIDE

The revolution is upon us…
    all over Britain people are dancing to a different tune…

Lights move behind my closed lids like a heartbeat, insisting something.
Syllables swell; lacerating every nerve with their exposed live wire,

changing shape and form, hoarse voices rear up from the dancefloor
as the track warbles *what kind of fool are you looking for?*

Nothing to do but slip in and out of the bass's womb, to lose yourself
amongst bodies bumping in darkness so thick you can chop it,

exchanging scents and extra slim filter tips, chewing gum and lighters,
the clammy embrace of strangers, the pummelling undercurrent.

Come, bear witness to this beatific vision – bucket hats and bauble eyes,
limbs fabricating abstract shapes, these underground Titans

kinetic as crisp, unclasped leaves, donning heat like a carnelian bonnet,
while DJ Kemistry, Jungle's lioness, sets the world spinning again.

She drops a dubplate, it loops, gyrates. I'm floating, free-falling – gone,
locked out of my senses.

    Heads bang.

        Eyes roll back.

            I bruise like overripe fruit.

Elegy for Buster

All black on black like a roadman
      he saunters across the banister

pads into far-concealed corners
      syphoning night's borders back

into himself. A line of ancestors
      captured in his spine's easy slink,

son of the panther, full of swagger
      & thunder, he signs off the day

with a feline nocturne, eyes gushing jet
      like a chess-piece knight

& the curve of his pink, granular tongue,
      lapping up semi-skimmed milk.

Night Shift

The estate lugs its weight in untranslatables;
your scoured fingers uncouple second skin
& limb by limb the seams become undone.
Outside, cats mewl into night's black brick,
bittersweet cloys tongue the way morphine
does, or molasses caught on a spoon's back.

We sit quiet in the planetary face of the TV
while an artificial halo radiates our temples;
you fan your bare chest with a medical visor,
stretched along the sofa like a black hyphen.

In the queue at Motion

Once again, a siren night. The air choppy
with possibility and foxes riddled with heat.
The queue's tide pulls back and we move
along with it, like a shoal of black sea bass.
Just ahead – a batch of glassy-eyed girls
braceleting their arms into constellations,
waiting impatiently for the gates to open;
for those first tendrils of sound reaching out
closer, closer, to where all language ceases.

At the train station a pigeon

squats like a miniature Buddha; loading a bullet
into his barrel-chested body, eyes fossilised open
as wheels roil and iron tracks wheeze.

Morning's wax sets inside the space he meditates,
turning his blue-grey feathers to iridescence,
a soap bubble amongst a nesting flock.

A dust aroma climbs from the train station temple,
from his dwelling's antique cavity, while the sun
slides down like a square of hot butter.

And he begins to preach in this strange language,
a hushed coo-coo-cooing as the world sleeps,
mouth gaping, closing, like a stargazer lily.

Day Visit at HMP Erlestoke

We're ninety minutes into our voyage and everything is melting:
lamp posts, car-wheels, golden arches, glossy liquorice wires
cuffing the sky, cut between gums of cloud like dental floss.

My pupils reflected in the window have become a gameshow,
caught in a soup of motion where the world and everything in it
has coalesced into this unknowable, unsayable grey void.

Then he surfaces. Past the jangle of cables, lights, and uniforms.
It's just our family left. Awkward silence. A single hug.
Curious, isn't it, how we find our inheritance whittled in skin?

Driving away – Corinne Bailey Rae's *Girl Put Your Records On*
crawls over the backseat, gnaws on something deep. Folkloric.
It settles in my eardrums like rain spittle, like someone else's story.

Blessed

Over breakfast the Devil came to me,
belching sulphur all over my porridge.
Big bristled hooves, forked tongue,
three blinding breasts – heavy, round,
the shade of koff candy twists.

She offered me a one-eyed lamb's head,
tight-lipped clam shells, a box of tampons.
Her nipples cracked into a map
of Southampton, leaked honey,
melted the cutlery.

She squeezed the flaming teat into an antique
goblet, mixed it with tears then slid it
across the table – *drink me* – etched
into its base. She tasted sweet
like girlhood,

peppered with a musk I had tasted before:
my first experience with death
when Play died, finding used needles
buried inside window ledges,
red inside white cotton,

smeared up the middle like roadkill.
Her flavour frenzied every bud,
like ants spewing wings, taking flight.
I felt one hundred hymens breaking
like bird skulls,

hips tumescent and generous as the ocean,
the smell of Golden Virginia,
baked tarmac, lemon Shake n' Vac,

the taste of Parma violets, crayons,
microwaved milk.

Through this mirage I saw mountains
of bubblegum taffeta, clear princess
tiara gems, Anne Frank's diary –
dog-eared, hair stuffed into Bic razors

and my first big-girl bedroom.

Care Bears stood to attention as I entered –
all white tummies, fat and full.
And my old rocking horse restored
to glory, exactly how I kept her,
with the bridle removed,

a box stood in the nucleus of the room,
inside smelt like pencil shavings, lilies.
Stay here forever, the Devil said –
braiding my hair with a coarse paw
as the goblet topped itself up.

I took a sip, kneaded into her lap
and let sleep take me.

Locusts fell from her cheeks.

The sun laboured a look.

Sleep Paralysis

The Catholic church from a few streets over
coughs up two, dull, dissonant gongs
and just like magic she unfolds on the third;
scuttles out from under the bed a red, naked nerve,
red as sealing wax. She's a flawless hunk
of garnet, featureless and blurred like a witness,
her facets casting shadows along my bookshelf,
the wash basket, the bed's edge. And as the clock
ticks and feral cats scream like delinquents,
she beetles across my groovy chick bedding,
staining the sheets with clots of red soil.

The sound of nothing is amplified between us,
stillness permeates like a hungry mantis.

What wound did you crawl from, stranger?

Leaving St Ives

The train crawls into the pied-piper's whistle
trilling from the attendant's mouth and inches over
the platform, coming to a soft stop

like an injured bird heaving its final chug of breath.

A woman pulls an orange from her pocket;
digs her thumb in to break its surface, the heart of the fruit.
She roots

under its skin – yanks up a spiral of flesh and peel,
newly naked, baptised by daylight.

The woman hands a segment to her just-babbling babe,
who grabs the crescent veined with white pith
inside her brown, bijou fist

and closes her eyes to sample its sweet-tart bliss.

At the window trees liquefy – meadows ebb in and out
like green streams as farmers dislocate their shapes,
levitating amongst the manure, the rakes.

I have become a Gemini projection, an artist's spoil,
some sort of changeling crafting dream-speak

inside my little blue book.

A poem

is a weird child, glimpses ghosts everywhere,
possesses herself like a fossilised shell –

gargantuan thing; sprung as an inflated lung,
halts life like a slaughterhouse gun.

In her hand the moon is a birthday balloon,
globe ironed to geode, the Rosetta stone.

She finds herself caught in time's invincibility,
suspended there, like a dog's lucid dream –

requires light to be seen, black–breath–white,
foaming space into primeval fragments.

She speaks in these extraordinary deformities,
music boiling blood, gold-armouring skin –

conceived inside the mind's squid-ink womb,
cloven-grown. Again, my water has broken.

Seal Island, St Ives

Over there – a harbour seal, pressed tight against the space
between land and sea, asleep under marbled salt –

hull wide-spread and levitating as if climaxed – mounting
the backs of rum smugglers and bookmarked myths,

laying inert as fresh cut flank or a hunk of Cornish slate,
eyes dilated into misshapen eclipses, bleeding pitch.

I wish I could be you – could fuse my thighs into a leaden
silken fin and dive in; naked, unashamed, gorging

on fish heads and crab legs as clairvoyance turns its hook,
dancing like black sea kelp in a spread of nothingness.

Oshun

she comes down
to the river at dawn
dripping peacock
feathers & pumpkin seeds
seven moons sit at her
feet like beasts or
men, their jaws
womb-pink

her bellybutton
is a waterfall
of copper wire
with full-bodied libation
she holds the sun over
my eyes,
calls the stars
closer –

water me!
they sing in waves
umbilical energy
rising like the tide –
like truth –
heaven is thine
& heaven is
mine

Self Care

Lowering in, I notice my fleshy parts transforming
under audacious heat: pink and slick like wild salmon,
a hot spring forms in my navel, cloudy rosaries
tack to my nipples, microscopic freshwater pearls.

Here I can fasten a nightingale's hymn into a poem.
Defy fears that have opened like night blooms
closing only when daylight breaks in –
I think of him and my insides groove like a lava lamp.

Limb by limb the world pulls itself together again:
no more, no more, shall I speak of my geographies.

HAS IT COME TO THIS?

Flying Ants

Once a year, summer appears to climax:

mud dries to stone – breaking open
        trenches zig-zagging back gardens
               & the muddy shores of city drains.

Flying ants emerge in the thousands,
        all fired-up like fresh conscripts,
              clamouring in clicks and fizzes,

              oozing spilled molasses, willing wings.
        One climbs up our bird-feeder pole &
bungee jumps off;

hitches a ride on a rare July breeze –
        wings ejecting intuitively & awestruck,
              his siblings follow suit.

Flying ants busy shrunken land fruit
        masked in red-black and antennae.
              Apples breach in the heat.

Pavement boils. The sun marinates.
        A tempest billows; clogging up
              the mouths of chimneys.

Some trundle into the kitchen like a set
        of lost marbles. People cringe & swat,
              squeal beneath their fingers,

even clouds go black like decayed teeth.

Fresh Set

Inside my local nail salon a red bulb hangs
like a hunter's moon in the periphery;

copper swims over each coffin-filed acrylic
naked from colour except the light.

I think I'll go for *Was It All Just a Dream?*
What a strange autumn this has been –

perpetual unease shellacked over everything,
over the ground and trees, the berries

rupturing inside mouths of honey buzzards,
over the table my elbows lean upon

now marked with snarled gobs of hot plastic
and silver glitter trapped in the fissures.

Time tries to cease. Nails dry in a river of UV.
She removes my hands quick quick,

holds them as if she's unearthed dead relics,
pushes in oils darker than tree resin

& nods towards her mastery. The cash machine
opens up – claps shut like a sarcophagus.

Outside the nail salon the sky feigns its reds.
The sun subsides like a dying cigarette.

I look down, watch three seagulls pick apart
a screaming rat until nothing's left.

A Woman on Shirley High Street

Behold her face aloft a too-big puffa jacket,
limestone ashen, pink eyes staring at me
before capsizing into sunken cheeks.

Today she's a coin-toss from striding boots,
negotiating a fix from some zombied kin
as her emaciated fingers stuff browned rock
into the cavern of a flame-lashed pipe.

She sets it alight with a practised flourish;
to evaporate in simplicity's sweet vapour –
to be lugged away, by the arms of some God.

On Grief

I barely recognised my best friend's voice. Couldn't register
such grave vowels emitting, or the sentiments shaking
out of her mouth, beginning, ending, in crises –

outside, outside, outside, she kept telling me. My legs had gone
gelatine, melded against the chair's hardbound mahogany.
You coming home? She probed, My mouth froze open;

darkness, plummeting, was all I could feel with certainty.
Somehow, the day drained. The sun couldn't bear its weight.
The pub fell noiseless. A chill hustled the shot glasses.

I grabbed my stuff and pried myself up, leaving that pub
an entirely new thing. And as water sloshed along
my cheek, the whole world turned inward.

Urban Kites

The sky sits flat like a heel-mashed bug. A red kite tosses itself
into the scene, leaves with a fidgeting vole in its beak.

In the kite's line of sight we're nothing more than figurines,
forged in plastic like Barbies, cosplaying in plasticine.

For a few minutes I watch a parade of daisies nodding along
to the wind. Something pulls me to pluck out Freya's

hallowed flower; to clutch its scant stem between my fingers
and puncture its green matter with a broken thumbnail.

The sky, dimmed and leaden, sits flat as the residue of a dream.
Cold as bone the wind seethes. Far off, a child shrieks.

Overhead, two kites orbit each other like satellites or lovers.
The vole carcass falls, lands in my lap bleeding, eyeless.

The Marlands, Midday

A baby's howl cuts through the shopping centre's drone,
into ears of people lucid dreaming like common moths;

in and out of this horde of shops manned by staff ossified
behind musty tills crusted with dust & dead gnats,

the misshapen fruits of the city. The baby cries out again.
His face is a beetroot flushed along a starling-neck,

swollen-up at forehead & reaching out, from the hooded
dark of his buggy, pale hand clinched – forming a fist.

Hot Sauce

The knife in my hand glints – brink up,
crescent body mottled by dried flecks

of Fairy Liquid, silver-paled in its curve
like the moon's anaemic fish-belly.

This tabasco bottle is a monolith bare
of blood. I loiter over its opening,

over sauce congealed in a maroon ring
around the bottle's blurred neck;

clots fluctuating colour where the fridge's
waning peroxide light strikes it,

a choker of tiger's eye. Aunt May's face
beams down her pride – *go on, go*

on, the butter knife is a guide navigating
vertically through this glass carcass

like how a humpback whale steers the sea's
upset bowels, its blues and blacks

striking sauce between flayed breaths.
Something in this hour turns me

greedy. I think it is the heat; how it rages
down the throat, sears off taste buds

with its tsunami of mustard seed and chilli,
crucifying me, in my mother's blood.

Bully

The slide is a yellow tongue: its steel marbling my lamb's face
into something unrecognisable, all mixed up and nebulous
like a man o' war coughed up from the sea's grey lungs.

We took it in turns. Feet firm-planted on fresh rolled tarmac,
sun-baked and stinking of summer. First the boy in front –
elfin thing, hair coloured to burnt wheat, gap-toothed,
beginning his descent towards the concrete.

Then, a spit-shielded finger jabbed inside unsuspecting ears,
lollypops and dolls kidnapped, the gavel of red bobbles.
Out of the way rat-quick: *slap! slap!* Strange mixtures –

terror   and glee   and omnipotence.

To Get Inside

First, Mum gets out my birth certificate:
a strange fragment slid out of lilac plastic,

delicate as Great-Nanny's underarm flesh,
exclaiming in faded Britannia-red ink

every inch of my undeveloped history,
edges curdling under a slab of October sky

as if pained by this newfound nudity,
snatched by the scary lady's anvil-hands.

Next zips un-zipped – our pockets gutted,
contents laid out in a mass burial across

a sturdy bogey-shaded nail-gouged table –
then down, down, to the menagerie of men,

to air clogged with cheap washing powder
and apple cider vinegar, the meaty balm

of Y chromosomes and sound convulsing,
coagulating, into a brief, desperate hum.

Vignettes about the New Forest

In the rock pool I'm something else:
      the river's bend, an empty shell

a nymph pouring a golden pitcher
      gagged by a cloud of gnats.

      Tadpole placenta fugues the mirror,
         algae mandalas trudge the surface

like a throng of boneless sea slugs,
      mucus-green and brimming alive.

The heathland's bruised hills detonate
      capsules yielding sweet nectar,

      maudlin moths tap out Morse code
         while the stars reveal their faces.

The world's fig-halves boil my chest;
      reducing to sweetened jam,

      thickset and glutinous and bloody.

Little Deaths

I organise my bag with mortician precision.
       The sun halves itself, a surgical incision.

Slide on a layer of chapstick, pull on my mittens.
       Overnight, the earth has toughened & my

boots beat against ground so hard-bitten
       I wonder if the worms are okay down there,

shut up in their glass skins, suffocating.
       It's mad how autumn sweats past everything,

deodorising the air with spiced pumpkin;
       mildewed windowsill, shelled conkers; all rotting.

I haven't felt this way since childhood –
       like a fledgling bird foraging for its first gifts

among brittle leaves, beak a black asterisk.
       I pull out my phone – another weather alert,

the sky wears her haze like a disposable mask.
       On a park bench I wait for cold to descent,

to pursue the shape of my cheeks, fracking each
       with red-pink like a newfound lover's motif.

A dozen berries collapse against the concrete,
       explode into these miniature crime scenes,

seven crows blemish the last dregs of light &
       the wind spits some syllables –   O
mother –

O mother –   I'm

sick

with these violences.

Pendulum

On a bench with a broken back
a woman smokes a cigarette,
the dog-end glows – ashes.
I am stuck in the city's throat,
nobody knows me here.
My eyes roam tarmac veins
& overhead, sky so saccharine
you can virtually taste it.
Stood in a charity shop's cavity
I watch it blaze & fade.
I see my Mum's cinnamon stick
fingers busy making roll-ups,
allotting them in tidy rows.
The woman's face appears
from the smoke like a prophet.
A pigeon tucks into nothing.
I offer out my hands to the cold,
here they are – open & empty.
Time drags her battered hems.

Spring Begins in Leigh Woods

When does a stream identify the exact point in time
it becomes a river, becomes more significant?

An alder leaf beetle scales the bark of a redwood tree,
turning metallic in the sun like a pigeon's neck.
The first scent of spring's fertility came curling up
my nostrils like a burning bundle of white sage;
perfume of damp wood and rehydrated moss,
sun-scent of leaves evaporating their overnight gloss,
extending the wood floor like palms turned up.

& somewhere the ear can't quite place, water surges.

SOMEWHERE BETWEEN THE LIGHT
I FEEL THE SUN

Leo Season

Summer, time to dress my margin with notes.

The earth smells like baby oil & muddled lime.

Skin pinks in the sun. Melts against pavement.

Dead-headed begonias choke between pages.

Loose clouds quiver inside the paddling pool.

I'm brought back to the copulation of thought;

how love knots my stomach like a hungry serpent.

Core Memories in Málaga

I want to keep things like this.
The heat of a retired day baked
into the balcony; reminiscing
about the Alcazaba, how trippy
it looked at the highest point
like a tapestry made from clay,
& you gave me some Bombay
mix, spice to take my mind off
the impending vertigo turning
paths of stone into tightropes
& vapour, candyfloss flavour,
forming strange little clouds.
But here, now, in the smoked-
light of night you could be a
piece of uncovered antiquity;
carved out from terracotta &
you kiss the backs of my knees,
climb up me like common ivy,
closing the space between us.
You say something about space
& a thousand suns implode. I
taste the ocean's salinity as we
lay down like two tablespoons,
tucked away in a dark drawer.

Strip Tease

From my window I watched afternoon spore
into evening, as the sun set about disappearing
over estates crammed in like uneven teeth,

above the heath of back gardens and scaffoldings
red-charged alive, ripe with the sun's waning,
that I watched strip, far off in the distance,

all the way down to a skinned harlequin sphere,
to a pulpy burlesque breast, a pink enigma,
in love with her diluted contours.

Recurring Dream

Something gyrates beneath my bare feet,
tuning me into its intuition like a vein.

Reddened rock sprawls along the horizon
in the shape of family; gripping the sun
with its many hands. A young vixen emerges,
scrutinises the scene with two golden
prisons of resin, two hardened pupils
black as dung beetle. She presses herself up
to the elbows in sand to understand it,
to know what it knows.

Solitude imposes delicious stigmata.

The sun breaks   into rust.

Remember

how we would listen to Mary J on our mp3s,
rinsing out *Just Fine* over and over on repeat
while all the grown-ups chatted like birds

of paradise in the living room, sunk into leather
chairs that reclined just so, how their twists,
coils and fros took on lives of their own

as soup yellowed with pumpkin was spooned in,
pillowed by thiccc dumplings that bobbed
along the top, remember how the scotch

bonnet would make us cough, its scent cutting
through the musk of close-quartered bodies,
clashing perfume, through the vague haze

of ground-green flowers that bragged itself out
into the garden, where we would braid daisies,
dress in our mum's garms from the 80s,

do dance routines and pretend we were queens,
how we'd sit knee to knee on the trampoline,
imagining, imagining, imagining;

a marine biologist for me and a singer for you –
remember how we were held ever tightly by
our truths, our limited understandings,

how the world seemed so far flung that anything
was reachable, obtainable, easy as two star-eyed
girls drinking homemade soup, just fine.

Lauryn Hill at Boomtown

I have nothing to offer but this image of my sister;
cut from the same material as our mother,
two-stepping on highland overseeing the Lion's Den,
shoulder blade glistening like a square of quartz
mined from the stomach of an old god –
laughing like a child under a small apricot sun,
sweat cascading over taut fishnet and stars of UV,
hues of every colour printed on polyester,
whistles and vuvuzelas, getting lower, going feral,
as spores of pollen flit like fae over her face.

Come Along with Me

I know a place   where pears ripen to belly dancers

veiled in the almost-blood-red you'd see slip from a recently powdered nose,
where seashells clink; reverberating every second or so like hummingbirds,

a growing echo. In this place moss-blotched cottages slink out of ground,
raised on their rotten hinges as if summoned by a necromancer's staff.

& the roof is canopied with ghost orchids suspended from unseen threads
like drowsing arachnids; with crystalline petals that curved into fangs
curving again into hearts, confusing the ambience.

Last night I saw stars falling frantic, inert as tadpoles, unravelling molten
alabaster while a young sun enamelled in its impression of sky.

I rendered myself as a gift.   This was all I needed.

Hooked

I am full of pack-rat tendencies –
hoarding image and memory
from the chewed end of my pen.

Parts of you sneak in the ink,
haunt the spiral of my fingertips.

Maybe it's a fragment of you
absorbed in these small notes;
the same but different somehow,

like looking into a marble's head,
a candle melting from both ends.

Dad, Eighteen

I love that you're propped up on one elbow
clutching a Rizla between forefinger and thumb,
bacci-slug fluffed in the centre like tree-moss.

Those pleats of skin stockpiled at the sides
of your eyes, who folded them for you?

Had you all mouth, grinning like a great white
sharing your spread of plinth-perfect teeth,
galvanising the flash.   A part of me

softens to view you like this; all cherub-faced
and adrift, faded into fragmentary browns,
when love was nothing more than a salve.

Hallowed

In this muted kernel of morning
I am a being free from body –
my roots tunnel into ground drilling
a dugout, reaching further, further
down, tenderised by shadow.

It's almost like a dream. A rook
opens up like a leather-bound book,
the sky shakes its rattle, seething
clouds that drop off horizon's edge,
foaming, spraying, white as sea.

My knees are pink from praying –
blushing as two queen conches
coughed onto shore, pores clogged
with dirt and multitudes of want,
permanence gnashed to shreds.

When did heaven taste like gnawed
nails or broken boughs of self
netting everything in a stone's blink,
luring in these cold barbed stars
and their dead-eyed yolk?

Far-off, life's bullet ricochets past;
day's husk fractures, frays to dust,
winter's dog says nothing can last.
I'm staying in the wind's numb bark,
please leave me where I'm found.

Bedroom Witch

Light a stick of incense and watch it grin
something maniacal – a miniature orange sun
strutting Dragon's Blood over my kitchen.

There are spirits trapped in our everyday items,
alive inside the ragbag of human offerings.

The soil in my palm makes strange markings –
bending into bridges with no beginning,
building into an unfinished symphony

and when I'm lone the air feels cooler; shocks
the tongue, knocks around the teeth and
when I swallow it starts to harden

somewhere far, deep, tacks to the gums, tonsils,
the palate like pollen. The world suddenly
feels nanoscopic and at last, I am happy.

A Memory

Sprawled out on your trampoline as darkness crawled in like tar.
My hand belongs to no one, a sleeping fieldmouse curled inside yours.

I told you things I'd forgotten on purpose, you spoke of childhood,
the odd meow-call of a mating barn owl sliced through the quiet.

Roni Size climbed out of a phone and our bodies became brown paper.
A handful of stars fell from their nebulas so bright they glittered.

I watched your pupils expand and retract, black as a just-pressed vinyl,
while crickets played out their samples, underlining the moment.

Roots

> You could see it in their eyes.
> Those ravers were at the edge of their lives,
> they weren't running ahead
> or falling behind,
> they were just right there
> and the tunes meant everything.
>
> BURIAL

Street life dissolves in the steel-cold
bass flows out like mineral water
becomes one with my blood
lungs part at the inhale
filling up with blue smoke
fingers stained with resin
pull Playboy bunnies from sealed bags
sound comes out swinging
so loud you have to shout
I spread my legs to the voracity
& the music enters me
strange nebulous melodies
filling me with breakbeat
as I fall backward through time
back to the beginning of everything

Free Party

Sound thrashes against its aluminium ribcage,
wobbles the ground like a phenomenon.
Shoulder-to-shoulder we move as one mass;
flesh-on-flesh friction generating elation,
an ensemble of carnivore voices.

Silver canisters concealed in the parched grass
twinkle under sun's lash like a bullet.
Above, nondescript birds form an arrowhead,
seeming to glitch there for a moment
the way birds often do in spring.

Jess hands me a plastic bottle of 'shit-mix'
blended when this still felt embryonic.
All over, tinctures of gold veer into each other,
vacuum-packed bags meticulously hidden
in tobacco pouches and secret pockets.

Something unexpected in my stomach's pit,
a primeval seed beginning to shoot.
I cleave my thoughts back to what this means,
butterflies self-propel throughout my body –
everything has started to breathe.

The aroma of antics washes me like a prayer.
A man with one eye offers up a balloon.
Herds of flesh trot toward the growling god,
popping up in circles, as if spores ejected
from the head of a giant mushroom.

Makeshift

At first you were just an empty grape punnet stacked with the recycling, lightweight but weatherproof; a thing that would last longer than me, long after me and the medley of birds commandeering our apple tree. I found an old flower crown from some forgotten summer, snipped it in the centre and looped it through the middle holes, where seven mauve peonies arched like a sickle, settling into newfound shape. Then came the weight – a rickle of robin feed, safflower seeds orange dappled by the sun nosing its way into my kitchen, raisins puckered to a leathery polyp, other pips, nuts, seeds, that I cannot name and a number of freeze-dried mealworms, favourite of the songbirds, turning with each step. No longer just an empty filmy body, but a body of matter transient as water, behind my hands carrying you out into the garden and up to the tree, hooking you over the severed branch, the stumped limb, which seemed to enjoy such adornments. From this vantage point, over grey mud forming my birthmark's likeness, over sleeping larvae moulting their former selves, I watch you, my new relic, being rocked by circling winds carried over from god-knows-where. In a patch of red sun a bumblebee tries out your infertile flowers. A blue tit twitches, belly full. More have come to gather now, to cling to you, unfettered.

FSC
www.fsc.org

MIX
Paper | Supporting
responsible forestry
FSC® C007785